Ogress Oblige

Ogress Oblige

Dorothy Trujillo Lusk

KRUPSKAYA • 2001

ACKNOWLEDGEMENTS

Thank you to Dan Farrell and Sianne Ngai. The author also wishes to thank the editors of *Front, Raddle Moon, Boo, The Gig, W*, and *Open Letter* where earlier versions of some of these poems appeared. "For D.M. Fraser," "Vulgar Marxism," "Sleek Vinyl Drill," and "Rumplestiltskin's Dotter," were included in the chapbook *Sleek Vinyl Drill* published by Thuja Books in 2000. Thanks also to Aaron Vidaver.

PR
9199.4
.L87
2001

Distributed by Small Press Distribution, Berkeley
800-869-7553
orders@spdbooks.org

ISBN 1-928650-11-2

KRUPSKAYA
PO Box 420249
San Francisco, CA
94142-0249
www.krupskayabooks.com

47827999

CONTENTS

For D.M. Fraser   7
Pity. The Greatest Aphrodisiac   9
OOPS UPSIDE YOUR HEAD   11
    Lumpen Prole by Choice —*a Novel in Arias*   14
    Cakes and Lager —*an Outré biografib*   18
    Contiguous Schadenfreude —*an Apocryphal Memoir*   19
    Funny in a Bonnet   21
    OOPS   22
Let My Voice Thud Throughout the Land   23
Vulgar Marxism   24
"We're All Friends Here" —*a Fiction of Unspeakable Horror*   29
Sleek Vinyl Drill   34
FRONTal for Jan Coyle   39
OGRESS OBLIGE   41
BOTul'ism (intra *DECORUM*)   56
Rumplestiltskin's Dotter —*a Meaningful Poem*   60
"Why Do I Have a Phony English Accent?"   64

FOR D.M.FRASER
Rich in Russia, owed wot an Etruscan earned

    & here it abounds
                    outstretched,
some rubbled *breccia* but
        mostly slick and canted towards the fundament.

    Errant friction fall-out
to repudiate a lineage
        of hammered patricians. A malison prehensile.

    And on the face of the earth, you were, exasperated and gentle
to the death. Condition of refractive wit, less the spirit. Buried and so
unlike your uttered element; integrating an invention, a story, a
drink, *supernaculum*.

    supervene the objective glut; precious, sold: solid by stratagem,
yet subsidence has shifted this plenum
    —and no more modest induction could ratify.

    Follow exigency with beer on the galleria of the exalted prospect.
How I could see the propertied outlines is blank beyond
wisdom thus, I've not
slept a wink.

    Follow the patter to reproach's pitch thitherward. Hawked
foreign sweeties at nut prices, could eat.

Subsequently,
the harvest required by insects
bankrupt rural estate

autobus=ATAM
shakes me upwards into small commerce, escarp, durance

  We are foreign birds yessir but quiet and stuffed.
Daily forages for provisions. Printer devil's lesser, coterminous
dogfight veteran as to social secretary, cram and borrow provenance
for expanded prowl across a darkling plain, over the Alps and
through the woods

PITY. THE GREATEST APHRODISIAC

chat a munch drunk party faithful
      colossal warfare
saturation bumming
  scab bands of happenstance

outré der fling

my job, *in potentia*
scourge, in polenta
venus dementa
a circular king, Divine, right of things.

                shirk some mummified
                cardamom pods without
                the necessary tool.

I am usually absent. I perceive the drift-by
shootings. I wander near your house.

the stellar averages,
an on/off summer stiffens.

        Clerical coughs up stickem
in triple penguin
—a complete Plantagenet
—a gorgeous chasm, an abysmal whole.

w/list of pertinents and a field of fodder.

       & dulcimer with charts and hammers
                       on order.

—a day off class. Casual sophistry *arroz con pollo*, saving
completed. Jaded whack of steam heads off sperm at the zoo.
Lose yon coprophagous rictus.

—Can I question?

Complete sense? Escaping the main conspiracies, I am set adrift.
There may be shunting, there may be unity, there may be elves.

—The beautiful music has stopped.

The nets entangled in the rail-ties. The level crossing—a labial
gesture and none the less fatuous, for all that.

—Undergrounded in realties. The older buddies.
The grumpy dwarf.

OOPS UPSIDE YOUR HEAD
for Maxine Gadd

early to rise comeuppance scissions daft hope within the
grasp of that gormless clarity of late become characteristic
of my finite state.

Face Be stated my Face

       Wonderful to hours—beldams merry mutiny ark's
an idea of Polis become an emergent feasible. Beams
as within facial experience
of eyelash intra Novelist's natal muddle like threatening to thump out
my giblets. *Pay Attention!*

Supply work as to that within rending a hammy adjectivor of such as
could be: accumulous, navigable, even
necessitous).(could surmise (one only may)
      piecemeal
    elaboration of munched up
and relic contingency, enclad in muslin & so nought of Nature's
museum, or
     that will I imagine

The Director within penury selects narcotic
mucilage, noiseless and rum. She skates that which may repel
in perpetuity, no grudge
None taken

Give me over mean interference to a pleasant redundancy

& Who are *your* gruesome antecedents, my Sweet?

    Let's white English!
Composing transits
of ineffable
Fluff

A fully evolved
mercantile subset
of Training Capital

He strengthens that which is marrow.
Your confession is my earth.
To me   you totaled soul   discards name
though being here.   Thinking out distant
     lighter that could fry
us up something
of the morning.

Lacking bread and brothers   seize fond sustenance
random Osiris magneto.

As I lack breeding and gravitas and degrees within the operation
of the menial forefront   the resounding grief and unlikeliness
while
gravitational rhetorics instill seminal prescience
     in waves find me
creeping
     at the edge of the trough.

I'm fixing to age   suddenly shot up I from
  out my
wit's end to a
   Belligerent and proactive
   e n s qualour ance.

This will do me nicely, she smirked
to chary Class mates

My Bonny Wee Light so soft, intransigent above the cooker—

Art thou troubled? Music will calm thee.

I beheld a vision
Of the 2nd Person, and I address You thus—Quack

Get out of town!

Jack Spicer ruined hell for the rest of us.

Art thou weary? Grace shall be thine.

Too proscriptive of vision's certainty, allow an anguished plea for every
sustainable circumstance.
Beholden to any Pothead that
trots down the pike. Meaning gets thrust
up every which way—
so much silage—I mean *"You know I don't understand your attitude at all"*
at all at all

CAKES AND LAGER
— AN OUTRÉ BIOGRAFIB

Mam I shrieked there is not any problem
Like strings of milt the clouds of early day foretold
More than I could wish to know of the fate of my
Father/grant application/demo/cheque/Dolphy tape/this
short-lived ornamentation has all but disappeared and now, within the
gloaming of my young days, beleaguered and bullied by american
spell check, I remain, Yours, an apparent whom

Mannered semblance or void aspect,
depose with respect to the nominally manifest.
Under jinxed survey of an all-too *soi-disant* intransigence
that over-fertilizes proscriptive peeks advancing unsustainable habit.
So shall I slink and approximate the implicit of an exhuming decision,
rather than what affords me.

Indemnity, or who I seem.

Signing off w/genteel daisy cleats.

*"I remember how fulsome you are and this has sustained me throughout
many a necessary condition."*

This won't get
any more amusing

A former cartographer, makin' a duck get sleepy,
reveals to me
that while hormonally
intriguing, due to my rustic forebears
and present urban penury, I lack an enduring trophy status.

> Incisor stretching towards
>> Baked apple gut
>> Bubbly slops, oho!

'allo whorl.

During the course of the job, I licked
many many envelopes
tasting of the slaughterhouse,
heedless of a nearby sponge to that purpose.

Crushing naturalized generalia, my underling hath placed the fff's
Back into gh.
You get yourselves
Into such argumentative states. Nobody thinks
To shut you the fuck up.

Passive voice (no suggestion), therefore incomprehensible
To that which could be my ultimate justification, sic love to
Demos, characteristic of an otherwise analytical mass.

Beer Girl, *Art Thou troubled? The slimy troll under the bridge*
he condescends so
prettily to
an industrialized diffidence, a feint then an upper thrust to the diaphragm.

The Lout (Ascending)—

Say

> *I don't believe*
> *that*

> *You wanna get up and dance*

Fragment (no suggestion)

Carouse with ambient lives

> My heart makes me think:

> > Tepid Phenomena all about us

Shitty old revenants, by starlight.

LET MY VOICE THUD THROUGHOUT
THE LAND
for Jeff Derksen

That which
we here embellish
is the fit of permanence

                              & thus may

I

                    recognize that persistence is operative.

                            Disorder, refute
                  and begrudge ME,
that which I am, today
                & arithmetical progression provises
en Code of Pleasant Muster for the bellwether mezzo-futurists saying
          "Get up off the floor"

&
I tend not to cite my source material,
so just do your homework and get back at me.

Suggestion: *He was cast in an heroic mould and his violence and self-consecration were alike on a grand, even savage scale.*

Or even: at godwin's they lamb holcroft and coleridge were
            disputing which was the better man as he was or man as
            he is to be give me says lamb man as he is not to be this
            saying was the beginning of a friendship between us which
            I believe still continues

VULGAR MARXISM

All hail the crushed amber groin of Late Capital refines
within extant character

That nothing will please me
any more
or any less.

& That I am dimly informed by the wry suss of the well-irritated,
humbly chilled of presentient ironisms Swiftly contained as to be
neighbourhood insurgent mechanix.

Well mays't thou throttle the percipient louse, the bedstead
maintaining
the absence of the full-stop.

Completely addressing the territorial aspect
of purgatory AKA bowel dressage—a testiculate device
whereby bummy
plants include stakeouts beyond sense declension
or shove under breath

GEO   PHIC   IONAL   Colum tailings

fortune incorporates factotum

                                    fetching ambient dread

in sheets, in sheets untied

GEO   PHIC   NAT

tinned Imperial measures and elbow room for archival vowel

Red Girls in sacristy—factor thus, shady spouse

face off in chains
garbed in perjoratrix enflatulalala easily
amiss of the swelter

     in funny bums of bees ignite
     in sinister missives, the breast of
     the likely gnat on Jack the
     Lad or seemingly harmless
     midges

For awhile of time past, in a glandulate
small factory, in an elastic confinement
—excluding argument, containing aggro-inducement.

In a small landscape—pathetic larceny &/or estranged
that which is sultry and flics away at theft under $2.00

sheepish thoughtly shmoos in monaural diversifications incorporating
'BLANDISHMENT'
'VECTOR'
'DESIRE'
'BODY'
'YR'

Up floats salmonid enhancement as
a sprightly effect, gnomic in dispersal.

After past retrieval
Justly apt shrinkage and drunkardliness
shoulder values
party lapses—animalian floral techtronics
sheet apropos goof
aspirate
PUNK SNOUT in LINSEY WOOLSIES
FINAGLIN' the DULL FINKDOWN MAN—
HOLE
SPECIES washing up of coastal waters—each shivery aside binding
co-determinate froth management.

                    SPECIOUS ASIDE, FLUSH RIGHT

I personally enter
recalcitrant SANDOZ, putter about shifting shale, consider
Cost-Benefit Analysis of Hominid Enhancement Project, retroactive
to the word GO.

Scheming little savours, collective glut
shove, Mighty River, shove

Folk art master comeuppance, quite rightly left
to narrate
an importunate cash cow or fuddled shirtwaist.

Shiny leaved myrtle
under extreme addiction
as when I was obuoy or mere slip of a deckhand,
I trod the undulant planks and lay anestle
in the drainy hold of this, my belovèd transience fidget, heft
awa barlwy, groats and unfinished fur.

I am convinced I have no father.

I am reduced to a generic being sniping at a hostile city-state.

LIBENS
VOLENS
POTENS

MULTO PLURIBUS VALE

Live in one. Put that mollusk on that throne. Onion share.
Stinky polystatic engorgement. In a preferred mode, the end rhyme
would best trick certitude. Could include cloth, may include
polyamides, wry bipeds.

Detractors of the designated hitter shirked retainer vengeance in the
shattered realm of Time's showroom *exegete. You are there.*

Sententious performance of Mighty word—I
want you all to give it up for Art!

Hoist allay avanticular horizon—go past astronomid outlet
camouflage FORTRAN, call off storm degradation

Million two Adirondacks encapsulated fustian DelPhonics
and thy potamus shall be my potamus,
whereafter a generation of lubricious processors piss me off

puritan potty mouth

I'm not just making this up.

"I am convinced that I love her."

I am poor and demonic and I've come to help!

omnifacet abattoir
misericorda

That which I have not

       misting stellate pinions and 'the Sydneys', given
       to sulks in the cloakroom, have not wished
       to advance, advise nor
       articulate the buzzy notion
         of tidy water sprites
         in pliant unison.

Her Highness's gots pudgy hands, don't she
    but you must take her nicely to
       wash them e'er
she gets her tea.

              dishes of visceral pickerel, a viceroy
O'fisheral. Salient tendency, brackish tenacity.

"WE'RE ALL FRIENDS HERE"
—A FICTION OF UNSPEAKABLE HORROR

gawking *about*
to case a 2nd joint.

Back it up.
Back up.
OK NOW

Time's bejingéd ferret. Miscreant
estate sale.
Tooling,
around in a Chevy II, cheaper parts. Half a sack and half a tank.
This's the accurate medical term for doughnuts.

The chassis of the mother embodying
the central contradictions
between means and relations of
production &/or sag of surplus value.

Much of the idiocy I embody could be ascribed to introspective drudgery, a slip-shod mop-up. Each and every sentence might just as well have stuck it out back on the homestead. Seems hardly worth the bother to write in the dark & strain a back out of locution, so to speak. But 'tis a poor carpenter wot blames her tools.

At the Building Maintenance Committee meeting, I propose the construction of huge ferroconcrete animals to bear aloft trusses of well-lit street signage, thereby affiliating public safety with a reinforcement of public perception that our neighbourhood is an Urbane Theme Park.

But to allow me the horror of *yet another recital* within a mutilated coincidence of relations and intimacy—I don't prosper from what I find therein. Find only myself typing the personal 'I' as numeric one (1), this quite the adverse of the adolescent's ostentatious 'self' effacement none too subtly signalled by the blatantly demure lower case & just when the poor little buggers could use a bit of starch in their *self esteem*.

But here and now are towels and bedding and bits of underwear that should best be hung on lines and are not.

Maybe some, like me, have snuck a peewee folding rack onto their deck to air-out sordid former washrags but probably contravenes Community Standards.

Wish to report on the atomization of the social under Later-Than-We-*Think* Capital as evidenced in the parboiled sphincter on each runner's abject gob, however,

they look *not bad* to me, but *do* consider the observator.

Any weariness there
is categorically different from that
of my former boon companions, carbon
monoxide wallahs all, with their
basiliskoptic glance of rheumy weltschmerz.

Lulu's barely predictable, entirely self-directed nap patterning has been denounced as a 'schedule' by another mum. Certainly I present within the public sphere completely wacked out & obsessive. I'm hoping I don't sound quite so bloody smug and self-congratulatory, but

I'll bet I do, I do

& I'll wager I'll witlessly antagonize umpteen other parents with everything I say, do or display on the person of my child. What a goof. I wish I was rich.

The Mummy's archaic corporeality is a remaindered sight of surplus value or conceivably, post-surplus ballyhoo.

> I've decided to become an equal, just like you.
> Here is my money, Now where's my mouth?

The flows of Capital and bohemia converge in these vincula of disgust. *e.g.* the pejoratific term 'breeder' coursing across divers artoid subcultures, so-called.

An ahistorical avant-garde verges on apoplexy at the approach of an active mother—RRRRRRR—. One's 'condition of being' as recipient of another's motive, rendering one mute or
mum.

Along with the rationalization of property
comes the rationing of the 'View'.

> A pane of glass appears to me on a six foot diagonal beyond my toes. The last light of this day violet and an opaque yet floral gold and I am so sad to behold myself within this brief reckoning.

Many theories could justify inertia's impropriety, yet, why not thrill to the tingling jests of novel modernities—vast oceans of raging enthusiasm in pacific concurrence of the most deeply internalized norms that pass as trivial nuances of a taste-based public economy.
—AR AR ARRRRRRR—

The pluck of goofy, yappy, over-personalitied public selves DRAINS and I am about to admit an error like an accessed visitation and so I dolefully make welcome, as is my custom. My word, in this sense, maladroit as over-extended.

I think I'll just make do with the tyrants as best I can, since it's much later than I think. I pray that the clackiness of my fingers typing, *non compos mentally*, will not now awaken my daughter, a titan bearing many legitimate grievance YO.

So nothing occurs to me

at any length, yet

I am no complaint.

SLEEK VINYL DRILL
For Clint Burnham

NON-SPECIFIC SIGNIFIED, new article

It is also interesting of dollars
a year
neither election nor
pissant severance package

your heath, my
sustenance, ballast of
thon hindmost grace

Eiderdown conflict but not for
manly yearnings of many years.

There's goats in
the Bible, (capricious tome
of traducious venom and bathetic foam)—but THIS is
the boy with the crumpled horn
that vexed the maiden
—all forlorn
that worries the cow
—all shaven and shorn
—that studies the house that Jack built.

       & where is the boy
who attends to The Word?
He husbands, engenders and butters the herd

up.

ur-domesticulate, spurious, may'st I espy
    such-like as distantly predicative
             but, like a poem—
          well-thought-out, worked-on
—to-be-honed.

                linking shot subjects
                to tree farms *system'o'neglect...*
                badger'd wheatfields

   reflected behaviours received mighty
       in holds of blood
he be fen-faced tho' cack-handed
       electorate pulsing, loving up some sylph-on-the-dole

  I also thought uptown wer'st several
planets about

      big shaman circumstance & keep your mouth quite picklish

beautiful

      half-grown slug along the pebble-dash stucco'd must

      be, that is to say UP in the morning. I won't.

Be that as my intention remains, muster grubbly manifold.
Inherent poetics will out.

   A worldly circumstance,
that likeliest nest of nettles

       —I must abound at hooves behest, a sufferance
of naval barracks. beans. & bars. & stripes without
a license. I chirp
& am left, bereft
& fecund

Are no further filmic cluttery
              bits of feeling stalked and staked
there was an now is not.

My liftless languor belies
             an urgent musicality
underlies the agency of
        obvious shifts

& clunky device.   A surfeit of contingency

blub blub blah blub blah

or post-labial fricative co-mangling restive
   &/or confounded lassitude
 of belly.

Whyfor be pleasure, measure of worth?
Why'st not thy fissure the very tantrum of a gallant?

or instanc'd of recoil an' weaponry—nay—sophistry
—raw coward!

Galimond sees the Dave.

More paleogentraic vocables, sluffing depictor while feeding outright
of ephemeral vegetation.

There are not here no milkweeds—
tiny birds of barky cellulose.

The expected is so insupportable.

Pathways to erectile muggage, shrugging legitimately through
sluice gated standards
thus culled from
the ever frantic repertoire.

FRONTal for Jan Coyle

You don't get off so easily despite time spent behind bars. Some of the names and places have altered the litigious. Fuck it flies. A knuckle sandwich the daily special LITERALLY.

In ways varicose and manner many, based on no mean or narrow purpose. About $7/10^{ths}$ down the page. As such, a frank and brutal capitulation to the house mix wherein there are no bodies to represent.

> for anything broiled by the body since
> it has as many which can be converted
> aren't they positive until just
> tender

> all day long, particularly an ordinary
> pan surface to some extent is in fact
> inaccurate in that this does appear
> where I produce

> are visible parts of the hair, background
> and collar studied are my bunny from
> what grew some composure under ideogloss
> is gross out

These are until you get AHOLD of yourself dammit. An obtruding territorial frequency that says it all, 'gets' lost and has a beer on account of the workers.

A melancholia induced by filth. Five minutes past a staggered flock. Genius is stupid. Art is expensive. Thrift is waste. Budgies! We don't need no stinkin' budgies!

your touching glass boss neatly caps
garage band bits to doubt myself of a
rather nice book for the massive event
of a best girl

is the moiliant nutritive of the opus carborundum
with whatever if is caught by the usual
necessities we have only just begun
to fit

formicary notes oftener than gestural regrets
or perhaps regressions of the mini-trampoline
of a snobbish heart I am always less
candled

The field is catapulted from identification. Reproduction is amateur. Hunger is sloth. You kill it, you eat it, you nominate it three years running.

OGRESS OBLIGE
for Michael Turner and Deanna Ferguson

Recur

It is, in the first place, yearning to this word, further on.
That which excludes action, and finds fulfilment
in subsequent mourning.

A guarantor, awakened by the shifting foundation
reproaches these pure products
of oral law.

The preferred form of
this imputation of fault

The "infinite demand"
            within the heart, or if
we see beyond the
influence of ancient
            prohibitions.

realization
, family
circumstandards
way to
"statues
into an
abdication of
of the will.
witnesses that
that direction by

Fearing alliances of meaning
without
taking immolation
into account.

A series of small, crackling sounds intrudes upon the contestable given of traffic. It's coastal British Columbia and rainy, however, there is a crystalline irregularity I don't associate with what I was taught is the Moderate Pacific Region.

sic transit seriopaths
livid *glasnost*, having quick become a hoary term
Time's anxious heteroclite
bombarding the sonar
engulfing
the gulfable.

These could be
organic sounds
belches, winces, (and
formations requiring
much water

fervent caste
        revealing pluperfect testament, installs
news worthy puffs and drung, somnolent
                        virtue

Much of the firmament
has washed away

present a grasp of finite qualities
        enfant de siècle, ma petite
too many stances intestate, current reckoning as an analogue of defeat

—recognition precluding disenhancement projection
what can be as enthusiastic as (justi ceprof ormo?)
your conviction disarms

pat an icon

E'en my soul awa, less tall rather testy littleshirts
bigger paths
you are not here you are
about to be provided for, you
could whine of shortlisted creation
an obit to arrange on arrival, constituting *this* poem
tonight scares some amply sacerdotal colloquia
—make me sad as a panda

If I could concentrate on my own provenance
I might just get a long poem

If I circumscribe
the difficulties
I might invert the order of my reception

You see no brilliance no longer
an apprehension of several decades, beneath
dread ambient milieu—all yours—get this
I can't see the figures for the desecration

A train sounding off
        (rustling remnants)
            overstimulated word
pushing this tiny knife through
    an end block of yellow cedar
hoping for benign intervention
        could only fork lightening ballasts

TOTALLY PATHETIC PHALLUS IN APPREHENSION OF CONTUMESCENT INTERFERENCE

forefront of climacteric threat
o'er the arched, chinook'd horizon, eventually
fitted up for 'equally vulnerable'
    (subsumed under social proximity
yon prolix autonomia

                        the reading of constant motion in
                              blatant disregard
                        of fiscal year in or Eurout

but this is not the experience of all
either belonging to a common
    institution

                        no business in the cold
                            ensnared rattle or piston
                        you are too early for this
or granted proprietary 'leisure'   connexion. The bus
whereby rain becoming   is taking this time.
snow can be   The attendants.
closely noted yet not   are intense. The articled await.
necessarily be written of
u r 2nd airy

legendary victim improvement

The snow adheres. Our ancestor's sanctuary is a frozen heck
bejeezus—a polysemous series of profane relations, same historic
roots (tho 't'were ten thousand slime
let the publishment fit the crime—"You write 'em, we pulp 'em"

—literally a social, intersubjective mirror—or perhaps flaunt of
suprajectivity, with an absolute vanity or iris vignetting entity to
scraps of convergent reflection, at least insofar as sending eggs and
glass containers crashing to the floor—we must constitute the
degraded character of my situation. Upon his rich background (an
agonistic manifesto) his manner of tenuous rhythm now becomes
wholly impressive to trial fashion into manly referenda.

(seeping into that homologous diversity)

see all and say nowt.

Will you withhold electrolytes, moisture, enclampment
dysfunction
shed fortune on the edge of shelter) contain,
itch, shift, meld the forefoot
rebuff
look-alike goalies w/hidden provenance
white transfer ware as investable
the massive molluskular discord
tripartict dissembled frottage at monopolic
Levellor, expanse
& *is* that an harangue or justified outburst?

In a blaze of over-extensive tropophagia
—back on the rack

my even-stepped *epasságe*, I grasp
—I will hangover, will be funniest

Have to save extensions louse you
acrid
Convocation re: bitter.
severe upstart loosed up
severest grout exhale pout restore progressor
project ambience

could string words, find goofy relations
get a bath, hold in my wreckage
SHUTTUP WOUND
stuck on an orange

you are small print outside an older order
There is wooden
amongst trouted treason
grassy plays to sleep with

WHAT A FRIENDLY GUY!
He may well have been
a theoretically 'funny' uncle
Enter all / wounds / all extant ordure
as excited would
as if the urban berm ahead (constituting my view/their
    encampment
    holding back the full brunt of aural thumpage, sirenage
    transport thrust
        self/battery rationcination planted
this id
never my decision—she'll go along, but.

(Receipt)

There is no rose of such virtue
        at your age then
        & mine
which passeth all regard

More likely fallen 'neath
        the jewelled crypt.

yon relegated mution

        lackey between
        gandy dancers &
        pitted enchildment

                        Position the limpid polyglot

Nor is there a falling of slower, thicker—as yon thicket opens up with
light, so
        a clarinet approximates upmost gender

She is still alive, grouchy,
                        disappointed, as if
                                appointment were ever at issue.

And now it is whitening the grounds and boards
—adhering, as she says, my meaning adrift
                                        in small kind (logocentrix) fixative
Will perish, will bust
Pallio-punative fire-drills plus more
inverted political homilies—should not I now chow
a whole faceful of phantoms? Thinking of smashing something
up, actually writing it, no telling what.
Few clinches are smirking to power or otherwise prehensile.
Did no POCKY fugate GLICCO
& take your dog away sooner

              World denigration and fearsome swells of proper
                                        Enhancement,
                            hinges on KETOSTIX
                                        fleeing the activity prod

U-ELECTUM—damn near killed'm

Tomorrow we go floating for trout. The lake is not endless, the days
get shorter. Some souls catapulted from *la vie quotidienne* were
lighting up the night sky. Flashes and flickers of recognizance
—tail lights of ghastly, albeit intrepid, weir fledermausen.

'We' is a time-biased brick shit-house
'I' is a trick-diving belwether
Some days you eat with hippies
Generalia extant upon reactive fodder
Lily fisting Homuncolonial clenching too viscous tints *en pointe*
in midriff rangette
'til
vaster sheltering cachepots
filter
through buzzing frames
and files of sentient
repetition.

He heaved Himself towards
a grasp of Faith's adjustment
—a shivering and tear weary enslavement
within homoousian homeostatistics   ooooh

Like almost everyone else, raising themselves upon these recondite,
littoral faults

> shiver me timbers
> plantation league
> cult mentality restriction
> forced on baseball
> amateur pissoir reference
> anabolic historicism
> resonance of salary escalation
> making white guilt work
> parotid child
> Bondoed glans appeal function
> speeding up the music
> scary flag budget

we built an earthen ring around our town failing to produce an
immediate solution

> Antilles
> be quiet

Composition

occurs later. deplete artifact congruence
nothing can be said
I matter in time fluttered cadence
for an ideolag, I'm deleted to pluck your aper-ature

He is onto their identity. This is a curse.
In general, this could be an *entirely literal* session

Smarm up or gut out—the browner belly line of pregnancy—whole
womb delays Sacristina editing means of propagation—renewal of
estrangement—paintings from stones.

Ticked off brethren. Velour enrobed matriarch of my imaginary
present—am I separate or sought in an adjectival squirm of over-
identificatory liaison?

Babalunar fisticuffs, stranglehold, choke chain, (bashed [probably
unusable] out of class consciousness) lacking in methodologie's
tidying rigour

You may exact sympathy, to your accounts.
My spoken style becomes her chosen arc of glamour.
A ream of erosion, lack-lust, a failed transity, plump and athrum of
dumb virtue, my naked lips, lank locks and puff adder acedie.

Stringent, yet I rather like the word 'hippy' and plan to use it again
and again in my work and keep 'tongue' 'your mouth' and my own
clothing away from it.

While many harbour lexiconic and should, could imagine, a graft or
two of occasional music, an unprincipled parsimony bookends that
which I must insist on as aqua potabile to temper this intrusive
expansion of mind.

My matter had to be more. There is solitude, over there. Mansions for mulch. I compost adventure tranx pummel Circadian sophistry go rise before dawn and damn the obvious.

It wasn't him. It was he.

A prefect (fucking hall monitor to the lower forms). This mum pisses Varsol. No more of *that*. I select an era and fit up the crampons. Don't talk back to my earrings you sultry bugger.

I am sticking to my sighs, a chariot adrift in the aether—though she meant antler and got all riled up.

Such are my succour grubbance. You all fitted up with calla lilies and al. Which aren't even lilies but usage.

You see, I disappear slowly but [Airplane joke—excise] don't piss mustard, also a whingeingly musclebound wrap-up. Combustible doily fiat an overlay of abstruse yet overly familiar jeremiad, irksome in its overtly defeatist model of the ration.

Dear Collective:

Borrowed 6 pack as aid to memory.
Will replace before next event.

xxxDotti

BOTul'ism (intra *DECORUM*)
for Aaron Vidaver

At rest, this upheaval: relinquishing

this/the

such

serial solidity of the
propertied callous
at the (throttling point)
hatchet edge.

Scattered forethought to
a scree of
bewildermenschanüng

stuttering plausibabbular towards
a future's gorm of
such, these middling days.   As if I matter, as if

as if satiated in

our tense agreement   you pull the clause,

  because

the symptom's

inattention.

        Listless

                in havoc, draw fast—you may not last.

Close inside of a dockyard noise.

                It's given,   instead of love

                        a flaunt, and

                present day Living Keith Moon, incontinent

        in an Holiday Inn swimming pool.
        "But how did you get here"? he asked,

        telling me where I was from: settling in my heart, like so
        many Ugandan

                        shillings.

Had you noticed, Christmas ornamentation

laying so close about Easter?
                    Do you walk slowly the halls and the taverns?

    Or, let's say you do ... 'n'othrs (another)   ...   strophé

in polite contingency.

        But, time for a story.

A few days into a coffin.

You didn't see anything.   Inchoate: blasted

          Porchival lymphatic
familiar/pheromonally plausible

            fugue

      Consider this intemperate

        creativity

That is Mister Man. Himself, that

Is.   From the men talking, it's not important,
                            yet good to hear.

        So   much   patience.   I haven't seen nothing yet.

(an embarrassment of lachrymose variance), whyfor, I'll not be saying.

            Inwhichsomever

                begotten

        an intracatastrophé budget & or receipt, includes doubt

(underlining) in a debutante's recumbent

                            slouch.   & ever

            so gently, he drew his thumb across the impressions

                        of his dead mother's fingerprints

                            in the long-dried putty.

RUMPLESTILTSKIN'S DOTTER
— A MEANINGFUL POEM

for Deanna Ferguson

As'm I depends from 'at mere-
tricious cons-
tancy of so-called 'blue' lobelia, Yes Ma'am!,
another these
       stinking shitarse fer-
       tile dirtum, yes it is

Amen

O the very first thing
that you must understand
Is a woman and a monkey
in a big brass band

       Mansions of Our Father
       Household of our Dads
       Time refines the present
       für die mädchen keine stadt

Dear Philbert Desenex, Friend of My Youth:

Yes! I do have six brave tits—but we have not yet been intro-
duced. Porsches's built by human hands—but your alter-ego,
my especial hero(!), has fashioned such this Funny Car
from Detroit stock.

Time deafens the prescient. I am PorkChop *del Fuego*. I don't
believe we've been
Introduced.

——————— Shiny teeth an'all—I've got SO much to eat now!

Big Ol' Plutocrat—You OWE me Man! Your cars
Aren't hygienic, also

So so much
By Fischer detailed dictum

I remain at length without license,

el Pie Man

The even yet disbanded Leisure Poets, so-called, discontinue
their anti-Labourian Past Mastery of *les Ouefs sans souci.*

Run Mild! Run Brie!

Do ye ken Jean-Paul
Wi' is coat so grey?

Leave off those interesting bicuspids, *hien.*

Fatal tenebrist, in the sense that a marriage must be played
from strength.

There is a catastrophe in the dishpan.

It is you who have initiated the process
& your travails retain an oblique lineage of
documentation. I've got to rise
to my Elvis Size—*without it boy I'm just
gettin' up each day
& walkin' around.*

I got me up every day
Got me nerf every gloamin'
Got a whole toto quantum
Meaning thus it ever was.

Within a white nascence state,
    the Great Mitch Ryder radio pre-
the Great Little Richard
    the Great Tom Rush radio pre-
the Great Bo Diddley & the Excellent Buckinghams radio pre-
    the Great Lloyd Price

You'd best clean ought
Your ears or there'll be potatoes
You'd might be hoeing.

& so more gloaminoid than
tenebraeic a sullen trough 'o' peri-
climacteric
funk. Thus it ever
were.

dotty-mouthed social self
emergent, rampant
In my dotage erupts from an hard-won
Sense that I need no longer
Present as Genteel. BAD archaic element.

Thus it ever was. AR! AR! AR!

"WHY DO I HAVE A PHONY
ENGLISH ACCENT?"

a kind of foreign white man abroad until fragrant funding gingers
and fondles
an ugh ugly
dull and indistinct Dominion.

> Into the seen frame scarpers a stinker
> Oh! you above a boy you!

What the chamberlain 1st lives to kill, we admit in our midst, rare
scary lessons while you guys are out—you guy

> former sonnets all for the plunder

this lack of consideration is commensurate, given a lovely sense of
Rod Stewart haircuts, a serene disemboweling of finer poetics,
cartoon woodchucks and me disavowing the beavers, ad infinitum.
Much easier to kill in a larger room. An anthropomorph-ed cootie, a
well-sighted bitch. A cleaner scope for the cleaning.

Thank you for going away for the week-end.

nothing
I am pleased. I like pruning and you keep away over water.
I am a happier instance yet wet of.

I am a mukluking Canadian about it all and quite nicely.

Is a toehold recapitulation pal big pal?

Up the mountain, toast flung. Better make it work, arsehole, subject
to literary qualities.